CATHOLIC SCHOOL *and the* FAMILY

ANGELUS PRESS
2918 TRACY AVENUE, KANSAS CITY, MO 64109
(816) 753-3150 FAX (816) 753-3557

ANGELUS PRESS
2918 TRACY AVENUE
KANSAS CITY, MISSOURI 64109
PHONE: (816) 753-3150
FAX: (816) 753-3557

ISBN 0-935952-99-3
First Printing—January 1994

Printed in the United States of America

St. Thomas Aquinas,
Patron of Catholic Schools,
pray for us.

Table of Contents

The Catholic School and the Family

I. Catholic Schools in Church History [1]

1) Introduction

In studying the origin of the Catholic School, we must take into account the fact that Christ was the great Master Teacher, and that He founded His Church as a teaching agency. Consequently, the Church established her schools for the purpose of teaching the doctrines of Christ in order to lead souls to heaven.

Schools have always been in existence in the Church and in society in order to assist parents in their sacred duty to educate their children. For example, we see the existence of schools among the Greeks, Romans and Hebrews. The Catholic Church, being the perfection of the Jewish Religion, inherited the Jewish traditions with regard to education. Thus the Church was naturally influenced in the development of her schools by Jewish ideals, especially with regard to the close union of the secular and spiritual life among the people. "As their main religious belief in the existence of one God, the Creator and Conserver of the universe, inspired their form of government, so it dominated everything else in their national and domestic life. It was so closely associated with their national spirit that to be patriotic meant also to be devoutly religious, the two ideas of religion and patriotism being inseparable. No nation in ancient times had so exalted an idea of temporal government; none surely gave woman so high a position in the family, or the family so important a place in the state."[2]

The Catholic Church, therefore, has always preserved this wonderful union of the spiritual and temporal orders among the faithful, especially in the domain of education. Of course, the Church was also influenced by the schools of Greece and Rome, and She naturally continued to draw upon the teaching power of the home (as did the Jews and early Romans), but when resources of the home proved insufficient, She established schools of her own.

As we shall see, the Catholic school has existed from early Christian days and it has enjoyed unbroken continuity. Wherever the Church went, the school went with it, or followed immediately in its wake. The Church has always promoted and safeguarded her schools, not only because of her general mission of education, but also, and especially, because of the innumerable vocations fostered by means of her schools. Furthermore, with numerous Priests, Brothers and Sisters to assist her in the task of education, the Church has always been able to provide not only inexpensive, but oftentimes free, education for the people.

Catholic parents, desiring to fulfill their sacred obligation to educate their children, realized that they needed to turn to the Church for assistance. They realized that the proper education of children requires not only those things necessary for family life (e.g., cooking, sewing, etc.), but also those things necessary for social life (e.g., literature and reading, the sciences, the arts, music, etc.). They, therefore, desired to do everything in their power to give their children an education would enable them to live in society and associate with their fellow citizens in a productive manner.

The Church teaches that education is not an individual work, but a social one: "Education is essentially a social and not merely an individual activity. Now there are *three essential societies*, distinct one from the other, and yet harmoniously combined by God, into which man is born: of these, two, namely *the family* and *civil society*, belong to the *natural order*. In the first place comes the family, instituted directly by God for its particular purpose, the procreation and the formation of offspring; for this reason, it has priority of nature, and therefore of rights, over civil society.

"Nevertheless the family is an imperfect society, since it does not in itself possess all the means for its own complete development; whereas civil society is a perfect society, having in itself all the means for its own special end, which is the temporal well-being of the community; and so, in this respect, that is in view of the common good, it has pre-eminence over the family, which finds its own suitable temporal perfection precisely in civil society.

"The *third society* into which man is born when through Baptism he reaches the divine life of grace, *is the Church*; a society of the *supernatural* and *universal order*; a perfect society, because it has in itself all that is required for its own purpose, which is the eternal salvation of mankind; hence it is supreme in its own domain.

"Consequently, education which is concerned with man as a whole, individually and socially, in the order to nature and in the order of grace, necessarily belongs to *all these three societies*, in due proportion, corresponding, according to the disposition of Divine Providence, to the condition of their respective ends."[3]

With regard to the family and home education, it must be said that parents must never neglect their responsibility to see to the proper education of their children. And even though the home is the first school, it must also be understood that it is not the only school, for the home is insufficient to provide for all the educational needs of the children who must be raised to live in society. Parents, therefore, have a duty to take advantage of the schools offered by the Church (and by the State, if the schools are not dangerous to faith and morals) in order to fulfill their obligations. With regard to the supernatural truths of Faith and Morals, it is the Church which has the first right and duty to educate the faithful. Parents have the right to teach religious truths to their children insofar as this is delegated to them by the Church. Thus, whereas parents have the first right to educate their children in natural truths, the Church has the first right to educate her faithful in religious truths, and in all matters connected to them.

Parents who are deprived of a local Catholic school, and who must avoid public schools which are harmful to Christian faith and morals, do a heroic work in educating their children in the home, or in union with other Catholic families, to the best of their abilities. But once the parish school is established, they quickly take advantage of the education offered by the Church and enroll their children in the parish school, realizing that in this way they will be able to fulfill their duty to give a proper Catholic education to their children.

"The home was the first school in order of time, and it must always remain the first school in the order of importance. The parents are the natural teachers, and in Christian society they are endowed with special sacramental graces to fit them for the proper education of their children. The home is the only school of early infancy, and in the past, the home was the school which dominated the real and vocational education of the child, leaving to the school the formal training in the school arts and in the detail of higher culture...

"The school is supported by society for the express purpose of ministering to the educational needs of children, and it cannot perform this function too well. But this obvious truth furnishes no justification whatever for the neglect by parents of their educational duties towards their children. The responsibility for the child's education has not ceased to rest in the first place upon the parents, and, while they may delegate a part of the work to other agencies, they can never escape the responsibility of overseeing their children's education and of contributing to it in proper measure."[4] The right of parents to educated their children is not an absolute one, but one dependent on the natural and divine law, thus subject to the authority and jurisdiction of the Church and to the vigilance and administrative care of the State in view of the common good. Thus both the Church and the State have a right and a duty to insure that parents give the proper and complete education to their children.

"The Church exercises her teaching function through the deliberations of her Councils and the formal definition of her dogmas; She teaches through her official literature and the decisions of her courts and congregations; She teaches through the personal life and example of her saints, living and departed; She teaches through her art and music, through the administration of her Sacraments and through her liturgical forms no less effectively than She teaches through her schools. The Church teaches through many channels, but the principles underlying her methods are always the same. They were bequeathed to her by her Founder as an essential part of the trust which works unfailingly for the salvation of the world."[5]

2) The First Catholic Schools: The Catechetical Schools

The first schools established by the Church were the *Catechetical schools*, which flourished about the middle of the second century. The purpose of these early schools was not only to teach Christian doctrine, but also to protect the youth from the errors and vices of paganism. Consequently, her first schools also granted admission to pagans who sought instruction in Christian doctrine for the purpose of coming to the Christian way of life.

These "Catechumenal" schools, as they were called, were conducted by the bishops and the clergy, and were concerned with the teaching of the doctrines and liturgical forms of the Church, and in giving the required religious and moral preparations for the sacrament of Baptism. Out of these schools there gradually emerged the catechetical schools which became the Christian academies for the teaching of philosophy and theology. Since they were usually conducted in connection with the Episcopal Sees, they naturally served as seminaries for the preparation of candidates for the priesthood.

As time went on, these catechetical schools added the courses of Greek philosophy and literature, history, dialectics and the sciences. The main reason for the introduction of non-religious subjects into the curriculum is the relationship which these courses have to religious truth. For even though they do not convey supernatural truths, nevertheless they do convey natural truths which also reflect the goodness and beauty of God, Who is the Author of all truth, both natural and supernatural. The Church, therefore, saw the importance to use all truths to lead people to the knowledge and love of God. She also saw the need of expounding upon these natural truths to refute the errors of the pagans who were using them (or rather abusing and twisting them) to lead the Christians astray.

The Church, therefore, while totally rejecting the false religion of the pagans, nevertheless sees the importance in preserving and utilizing whatever is good in their art, in their philosophy, in their literature and in their education. For everything which is true or good should be used by Christians to give glory to God. Thus, even though the primary purpose of the Catechetical schools was to teach the truths of faith and morals revealed by Christ and taught by the Church, nevertheless the other non-religious subjects of learning were added to the curriculum by the Church, and modified at various times in accordance with the needs of the Church and society.

As the conflict between Christianity and pagan philosophy gave rise to catechetical schools, so the more general struggle between Christian and pagan standards of life gave rise to other provisions on the part of the Church for safeguarding the faith of Christian children. In the first centuries, great stress was laid on the importance of home education, and this task was committed in a special manner to Christian mothers, who had to counteract the influence of pagan schools on their children. There were also private schools for Christian youth taught by Christians.

3) The Monastic Schools

In the fourth century, *Monastic schools* came into being as a reaction against the corrupt standards of paganism which were beginning to influence Christians, not only in their public life, but also their private and family life. It was St. Basil who organized monastic life in the East towards the end of the fourth century. He suggested that the monks should take up the work of instructing both children and adults. He also commended the practice of not confining instruction to the Scriptures. In his address to young men on the right use of Greek literature, he says: "So we, if wise, shall take from heathen books whatever befits us and is allied to the truth, and shall pass over the rest."[6]

St. John Chrysostom also testifies to the decline of fervor among Christian families at the end of the fourth century. He saw that the family was no longer able to provide a proper religious and moral training for the children in the home. Consequently, he told parents that if they could not provide a Christian training in the home, then they must send their children to the monasteries, even though by so doing they would have to sacrifice their higher literary training. He says: "In fact, the choice lies between two alternatives; a liberal education which you may get by sending your children to the public schools, or the salvation of their souls which you secure by sending them to the monks. Which is to gain the day, science or the soul? If you can unite both advantages, do so by all means; but if not, choose the more precious."[7]

4) Cathedral Schools and the Schola Cantorum, or Chantry Schools

From this period up to the time of Charlemagne (5th - 9th century), Christian education was imparted in the *Cathedral schools* and the *Chantry Schools*, or *Schola cantorum,* which came to be associated with each Episcopal See. The Cathedral Schools sprang from the Episcopal schools which existed from a very early time in the Church for the training of clerics.[8] The bishop himself had control over the school, and under him was the school's immediate superior, the *Magister scholae*. In the cities and towns where there was no cathedral, the canons of the local church conducted a "canonicate" school.

"In both institutions there were distinguished two levels of education: 1) the elementary school (schola minor) where reading, writing, psalmody, etc., were taught; and 2) the higher school (schola maior), in which the curriculum consisted either of the trivium alone (grammar, rhetoric, and dialectic), or of the full programme, namely the seven liberal arts, Scripture, and what we now call pastoral theology. The method employed in the Cathedral schools was identical with that of the monastic schools."[9]

"The *Chantry schools* were similar in character to the cathedral and canonicate schools. Indeed, they may be said to be a specific kind of canonicate school. The Chantry was a foundation with endowment, the proceeds of which went to one or more priests carrying the obligation of singing or saying Mass at stated times, or daily, for the soul of the endower, or for the souls of persons named by him. It was part of the duty of the incumbents of a Chantry foundation to 'teach gratis the poor who asked it humbly for the love of God'."[10]

5) Guild Schools, Hospital Schools and City (Parish) Schools

The Guild schools, Hospital Schools and City Schools, the last beginning with the thirteenth century, shared the work of education with the monastic, cathedral and Chantry schools. The *guild and hospital schools* were ecclesiastical foundations. They were guided by clerics, and engaged in the work of education under the direction of the Church. The *city schools (parish schools)*, which were also under the control of the Church, at first met with opposition from the teachers in the monastic and cathedral foundations.[11]

"In *Parish schools*, which offered elementary education to the children of the people, and in the great *monastic schools*, which offered education both to the laity and to those who intended to enter the monastic orders, St. Benedict taught the dignity of labor and the arts of peace. These schools were all created and supported by the Church. In some instances, fees were paid by the pupils, but in many cases the education was entirely free."[12]

6) Charlemagne: The Catholic State and Education

It was Charlemagne who commissioned the State to assist in an official manner in Christian education. He perfected the palace school by appointing Alcuin as minister of education of the Empire. "The genius of Charlemagne was shown not merely by the number of subjects he had won or the width of territory he had subdued, but also by his zeal for the internal development of the empire, above all in the matter of education. He gathered round him a cycle of scholars who were meant to be the tutors of his rough subjects, and he himself was the noblest and most enthusiastic pupil of them all. The English scholar, Alcuin (735 - 804) was above all his mentor and counselor: a man of varied learning, whose works, deep for that uncultured age, still stand side by side with those of Bede and others in the Latin Patrology. Alcuin had been trained in the School of York established by Egbert, second metropolitan of that See, and had besides this gone to Rome, where he drank deeply of the traditions of the Church. He was the Master of the Palace School of the Frankish monarch, and was able to train scholars who after wards filled high places in the Church and State."[13]

Charlemagne also urged the abbots and bishops to do everything in their power to effect Christian education among the people. In response, the abbots and bishops saw to the establishment of free schools in many cities, and monastic schools, in many instances, offered free room and board as well as free instruction. Alfred the Great exerted a similar influence on the schools of England.[14]

"The Carlovingian revival of education affected not only the internal schools of the monasteries, but also the external schools, and during the reign of Charles' successors, bishops and popes by a number of decrees shoed their interest in the maintenance not only of schools of sacred science, but also in schools 'for the study of the letters'."[15]

"The education of women was also provided for in the convents for women, and by the nuns who frequently conducted schools for the young boys and girls in the villages and cities where they were located. The sons of the nobility, from the age of seven or eight, were trained in the palaces of the feudal lords. Under the favor and with the assistance of both church and state, schools were multiplied throughout Christendom. They grew in excellence and were shaped into system by the scholastics."[16]

7) The Middle Ages and Education

"The Church, during the Middle Ages, controlled education in all Christian countries. It was through Her authority that schools were built, that teachers were licensed, the elements of the curriculum were determined, and, while she always utilized the school for the religious education of her children, and for the special preparation of her priests, She did not confine the scope of the school to these aims. The generous impulses of her conscious life nourished into vigor all the capacities and faculties of man.

"Through her liturgy and her organic teaching, She quickened the aesthetic sense and furnished inspiration and guidance to the fine arts. Music, painting, sculpture, manuscripts, ornamental metal work, poetry and literature were all encouraged and supported by her, while in her monastic schools she taught the children of the people agriculture and the industrial arts."[17]

"The interests of both the Church and the State were promoted by schools whose aim was to develop Christian virtues no less than to impart skill in the arts, and knowledge of literature, theology, philosophy and the sciences. Naturally, therefore, education continued to spread among the people and schools to multiply until the Protestant Reformation checked the movement by confiscating the funds of bishoprics and monasteries, and exciting the people to break away from the influence of the Church."[18]

8) Catholic Schools in American History

The oldest schools in America are the Catholic schools founded about 1600 in the Spanish colonies. The French colonies, too, had their schools as a regular part of the civil and religious work of colonization. Catholic educational work in the Thirteen colonies dates from the arrival of the Catholic colony in Maryland. The first regularly established school in Maryland dates from 1640.

"The earliest Catholic colonists implanted the principle of religious training in the virgin Catholic soil, and every decade that has passed since then has added but a new growth or a fresh vigor to the educational mustard seed. A school appears to have been founded by the Jesuits in Maryland not long after the arrival of the first colonists, though there is some uncertainty as to the exact date and its first location. But even before the coming of the Calverts, Catholic schools existed in New Mexico and Florida. By the year 1629, many schools for the natives of New Mexico had been established by the Franciscans, and this was eight years before the first school in the thirteen eastern colonies. The first schools within the present limits of the United States were thus founded by Catholic missionaries."[19]

As the condition changed from that of a missionary country to that of a country with complete ecclesiastical organization, the schools came to be recognized as a function of organized parish work. In the Spanish and French colonies, the school like the Church looked to the State for support. In the English colonies, there was also State support of denominational education, but whether the Catholics could or could not secure a share of the public funds depended on local conditions.

Thus, during the Colonial period in the United States, and for a considerable time thereafter, the main force in establishing schools came from the Catholic missionaries. The Catholic schools throughout the colonies were chiefly taught by priests who later on brought to their assistance religious teaching communities of men and women. But there was great difficulty in providing teachers for the schools. The pastor frequently taught the school himself, and when his other duties became too numerous, he employed Catholic laymen and women for the work. In the missions conducted by religious communities, the conduct of the school was an easier matter, as the teachers were supplied by the communities. In the course of time, various religious orders were established in the United States for the work of Catholic education. They greatly assisted the priest in the schools, and through their efforts, Catholic schools rapidly multiplied throughout the States.

The American Protestants were not able to provide such an efficient means of education for their children, for they did not have the religious communities from which to draw as the Catholic Church did. This caused great concern among them, and even led to bitter persecution against Catholics and the Catholic Schools. The widespread hatred for Catholicism was especially revealed in the writings of the famous Boston Presbyterian clergyman, Rev. Lyman Beecher, who said: "If we do not provide the schools which are requisite for the cheap and effectual education of the children of the nation, it is perfectly certain that the Catholic powers of Europe intend to make up the deficiency, and there is no reason to doubt that they will do it, until, by immigration and Catholic education, we become to such an extent a Catholic nation, that with their peculiar power of acting as one body, they will become the predominant power of the nation."[20]

For a long time both Catholic and Protestant schools frequently received assistance from public funds. The non-denominational schools were controlled by the Public School Society. In 1824, state support was withdrawn from denominational schools, mainly through the work of the Public School Society. In 1840, a great controversy arose in New York, after Governor Seward's message to the Legislature (on Jan. 1), in which he declares that religion should not be taught in the public schools for fear of promoting any individual religious denomination. This controversy between the Catholics and non-Catholics of New York led to the discontinuance of the Public School Society, and the establishment of the state school system. The Catholic Church immediately called for the establishment of parish Catholic schools for the proper education of Catholics. From 1840 on, state schools also were rapidly developed throughout the country.

"The state schools are supported by the taxes paid by Catholic and non-Catholic alike. When the public support was withdrawn from Catholic schools, the Church addressed herself at once to the onerous task of building up a school system of her own in which Catholic immigrants might be taught in their own language and in which the secure foundations of the Catholic faith might be laid. During the fourscore years that have elapsed, She has continued her work of education in her schools, not because she denies the right of the state to instruct its citizens, but she regards the training of every man and woman in the truths of religion a matter of paramount importance, both for temporal and for eternal welfare."[21]

II. Papal Teachings on Education

1) "Education is essentially a social and not merely an individual activity. Now there are three essential societies, distinct one from the other, and yet harmoniously combined by God, into which man is born: of these, two, namely the family and the civil society, belong to the natural order. In the first place comes the family, instituted directly by God for its particular purpose, the procreation and the formation of offspring; for this reason, it has priority of nature, and therefore of rights, over civil society.

"Nevertheless the family is an imperfect society, since it does not in itself possess all the means for its own complete development; whereas civil society is a perfect society, having in itself all the means for its own special end, which is the temporal well-being of the community; and so, in this respect, that is in view of the common good, it has pre-eminence over the family, which finds its own suitable temporal perfection precisely in civil society.

"The third society into which man is born when through Baptism he reaches the divine life of grace, is the Church; a society of the supernatural and universal order; a perfect society, because it has in itself all that is required for its own purpose, which is the eternal salvation of mankind; hence it is supreme in its own domain.

"Consequently, education which is concerned with man as a whole, individually and socially, in the order to nature and in the order of grace, necessarily belongs to all these three societies, in due proportion, corresponding, according to the disposition of Divine Providence, to the condition of their respective ends.

"First of all, education belongs pre-eminently to the Church, by reason of a double title in the supernatural order, conferred exclusively upon her by God Himself; absolutely superior therefore to any other title in the natural order. The first title is founded upon the express mission and supreme authority to teach, given her by her divine Founder (Mt. 28: 18-20)... The second title is that of supernatural motherhood, in virtue of which the Church, spotless spouse of Christ, generates, nurtures and educates souls in the divine life of grace, through her sacraments and her doctrine. With good reason then does St. Augustine maintain: 'He has not God for Father who refuses to have the Church as mother.'"[22]

2) "Right from the most ancient times, Christian parents have always understood that it was their duty and also to their interest to profit from that treasury of Christian education that the Church puts at their disposition. Thus at all times, Christian families, fathers and mothers, came knocking on behalf of their children on the doors of the schools and the educational institutions offering Christian education. These most beautiful truths eloquently demonstrate two facts of great importance: that of the Church, placing at the disposal of families her office of mistress and educator, and of families, eager to profit by the offer, and entrusting their children to the Church in hundreds and thousands. And these two great facts recall and proclaim a striking truth of the greatest significance in the moral and social order. They declare that the mission of education regards before all, and above all, *primarily the Church and the family*, and this by natural and divine law, and that therefore it cannot be slighted, cannot be evaded, cannot be supplanted."[23]

3) "This educational environment of the Church embraces the Sacraments, the divinely efficacious means of grace; the sacred Ritual, so wonderfully instructive; and the material structure of her churches, whose liturgy and art have an immense educational value; but it also includes the great number and variety of schools, associations and institutions of all kinds, established for the training of youth in Christian piety, together with literature and the sciences, not omitting recreation and physical culture.

"And in this inexhaustible fecundity of educational works, how marvelous, how incomparable is the Church's maternal providence! So admirable, too, is the harmony which she maintains with the Christian family, that the Church and the family may be said to constitute together one and the same temple of Christian education."

"Since, however, the younger generations must be trained in the arts and sciences for the benefit and prosperity of civil society, and since the family of itself in unequal to carry out this task, it was necessary to create that social institution, the school. But let it be borne in mind, that this institution owes its existence to the initiative of the family and of the Church, long before it was undertaken by the State. Hence, considered in its historical origin, the school is by its very nature, an institution subsidiary and complementary to the family and to the Church."[24]

4) "Logically it should be recognized that the full and perfect task of teaching belongs not to the State but to the Church, and that the State cannot prevent her from fulfilling this duty, nor can it reduce it to a tacit teaching of the religious truths. No damage can be done in this way to the true and proper rights, or rather, the duties of the State, as regards the education of its citizens.

"The State has nothing to fear from the education given by the Church and under her directives; it is this education that has given substance to modern civilization insofar as concerns what it now possess of good.

"The family at once realized that such is the case, and from the Church's very first days right through the ages of our times, fathers and mothers, even if weak or non believers, sent their sons by the millions to the educational institutions founded and directed by the Church."[25]

5) "In the matter of education, it is the right, or to speak more correctly, it is the duty of the State to protect by means of its legislation the prior rights already described of the family as regards the Christian education of its offspring, and consequently also to respect the supernatural rights of the Church in this same realm of Christian education.

"It is also the duty of the State to protect the rights of the child itself when the parents are found wanting, either physically or morally in this respect, whether by default, incapability or misconduct, since, as has been shown, their right to educate is not an absolute and despotic one, but dependent on the natural and divine law, and therefore subject to the authority and jurisdiction of the Church, and to the vigilance and administrative care of the State in view of the common good. Besides, the family is not a perfect society, that is to say, it has not in itself all the means necessary for its full development. In this case, an exceptional one no doubt, the State does not take the place of the family, but merely makes provision for its deficiencies, and provides suitable means, always in conformity with the natural rights of the child and the supernatural rights of the Church."[26]

6) "In the first place, it pertains to the State, in favor of the common good, to promote in various ways the education and instruction of youth. It should begin by encouraging and assisting, of its own accord, the initiative and activity of the Church and the family, whose successes in this field have been clearly demonstrated by history and experience. It should, moreover, supplement their work whenever this falls short of what is necessary, even by means of its own schools and institutions. For the State, more than anyone else, is provided with the means put at its disposal for the needs of all, and it is only right that it should use these means to the advantage of those who have contributed thereto.

"Over and above this, the State can exact and take means to secure that all its citizens have the necessary knowledge of their civil and political duties, and a certain degree of physical, intellectual and moral culture, which, considering the conditions of our times, is really necessary for the common good.

"However, it is clear that in all these ways of promoting education and instruction, both public and private, the State should respect the inherent rights of the Church and of the family, and moreover have regard for distributive justice. Accordingly, unjust and unlawful is any monopoly, educational or scholastic, which, physically or morally, forces families to make use of government schools, contrary to the dictates of their Christian conscience, or contrary even to their legitimate preferences.

"This does not prevent the State from making due provision for the right administration of public affairs and for the protection of its peace, within or without the realm. These are things which directly concern the public good and call for special aptitudes and special preparation. The State may, therefore, reserve to itself the establishment and direction of schools intended to prepare for certain civic duties and especially for military service, provided it be careful not to injure the rights of the Church or of the family in what pertains to them...

"In general also it belongs to civil society and the State to provide what may be called civic education, not only for its youth, but for all ages and classes. This consists in the practice of presenting publicly to groups of individuals information having an intellectual, imaginative and emotional appeal, calculated to draw their wills to what is upright and honest, and to urge its practice by a sort of moral compulsion, positively by disseminating such knowledge, and negatively by suppressing what is opposed to it. This civic education, so wide and varied in itself as to include almost every activity of the State intended for the public good, ought also to be regulated by the norms of rectitude, and therefore cannot conflict with the doctrines of the Church, which is the divinely appointed teacher of these norms."[27]

7) "The Apostolate for the holy education of girls is a present-day necessity: it is urgently needed to awaken the Christian spirit among the masses and to assist women to be for humanity, with the gifts they have from nature and grace, instruments not of ruin but of conversion and salvation."[28]

8) "The State is obliged to take a vital interest in the education of its citizens; however, it does so only in that it aids the individual and the family in all that they cannot do of themselves. The State is not made to absorb, to engulf and to annihilate the individual and the family; that would be ridiculous, it would be contrary to nature in that the family precedes the State and society. The State cannot neglect the question of education but must contribute and procure what is necessary and sufficient to help, to cooperate and to perfect the efforts of the family, to correspond entirely with the desires of the father and mother, and above all, to respect the divine right of the Church."[29]

9) "Training in the home, however wise, however thorough, is not enough. It needs to be supplemented and perfected by the powerful aid of religion. From the moment of Baptism, the priest possesses the authority of a spiritual father and a pastor over your children. You must cooperate with him in teaching them the first rudiments of the catechism and the piety which are the only basis of a solid education...

"In your work of education, which is many-sided, you will feel the need and the obligation of having recourse to others to help you. Choose helpers who are Christians like yourselves, and choose them with all the care that is called for by the treasure that you are entrusting to them. When you have chosen them, you must not think that you are henceforth freed from your duty and your vigilance. You must cooperate with them. However eminent school teachers may be in their professions, they will have little success in the formation of your children without your collaboration. Even less will they have if instead of helping and lending support to their efforts you were to counteract and oppose them."[30]

10) "False also and harmful to Christian education is the so-called method of *'co-education'*. This too, by many of its supporters, is founded upon naturalism and the denial of original sin; but by all, upon a deplorable confusion of ideas that mistakes a leveling promiscuity and equality, for the legitimate association of the sexes. The Creator has ordained and disposed perfect union of the sexes only in matrimony, and, with varying degrees of contact, in the family and in society. Besides, there is not in nature itself, which fashions the two quite different in organism, in temperament, in abilities, anything to suggest that there can be or ought to be promiscuity, and much less equality, in the training of the two sexes. These, in keeping with the wonderful designs of the Creator, are destined to complement each other in the family and in society, precisely because of their differences, which therefore ought to be maintained and encouraged during their years of formation, *with the necessary distinction and corresponding separation*, particularly in the most delicate and decisive period of formation, that, namely, *of adolescence*."[31]

11) "The Sacred Congregation is, moreover, aware of the fact that there can be given circumstances in which Catholic parents, can, with a clear conscience, send their children to public schools; but in order to do so, an adequate motive is needed, and it must be left to the conscience of the bishops whether there exists sufficient motive or not in any given case; according to what has already been said, sufficient reason will exist if there are no Catholic schools, or if those which already exist are not adapted to train

adolescents according to their condition in life...

"So that these public schools can be attended with a clear conscience, however, the danger of perversion, which is always more or less inherent in the very system of these schools, must be warded off with suitable precautions. It must be ascertained whether, in the school to be attended the danger of perversion is of such a nature that its evil effects are unavoidable, if the daily things that are taught and done are contrary to Catholic teaching and morality and cannot fail to cause spiritual injury. Such a danger must, quite obviously, be absolutely avoided, at the cost of any sacrifice whatsoever, even that of life.

"So that children may, with a clear conscience, be entrusted to the public schools, they should receive the necessary Christian instruction and education in the most suitable manner outside school hours. Remembering, therefore, what the Council of Baltimore very prudently decided on this matter, parish priests and missionaries will teach catechism with great attention and will take special care to explain the truths of the Faith and of morals that are being opposed by the incredulous and the heterodox, and they will make careful and zealous efforts to impart strength to the young people who are exposed to so many dangers and will spur them on without respite to preserve their religion by means of frequent approach to the Sacraments, and by special devotion to the Blessed Virgin Mary.

"Parents, or those taking their place, should guard their children most carefully and should question them on the lessons they have attended; they should examine the books that have been issued and, if they find in them anything that is injurious, they should counteract its effects; finally, they should separate them absolutely and preserve them from all familiarity and intimacy with fellow students who are capable of endangering their Faith or habits, and from those whose behavior is depraved.

"This instruction and this necessary Christian education of their children is often neglected by those parents who allow their children to frequent schools where it is impossible to avoid the loss of souls or who, notwithstanding the existence of a well-organized neighboring *Catholic school* or the possibility of having their children educated elsewhere in a *Catholic School*, entrust them to public schools *without sufficient reason* and *without having taken the necessary precautions to avoid the danger of perversion*; it is a well-known fact that, according to Catholic moral teaching, *such parents*, should they persist in their attitude, *cannot receive absolution in the Sacrament of Penance*."[32]

12) "We renew and confirm their (Pius IX and Leo XIII) declarations, as well as the Sacred Canons, in which the frequenting of non-Catholic schools, whether neutral or mixed, those namely which are open to Catholic and non-Catholics alike, is forbidden for Catholic children, and can be at most tolerated on the approval of the Ordinary alone, under determined circumstances of place and time, and with special precautions."[33]

This decree is but a paraphrase of the general law of the Church as expressed in Canon 1374: "Catholic children must not attend non-Catholic, neutral or mixed schools, that is, such as are also open to non-Catholics. It is for the bishop of the place alone to decide, according to the instructions of the Apostolic See, in what circumstances and with what precautions attendance at such schools may be tolerated, without danger or perversion to the pupils."

III. Ecclesiastical Decrees in the United States

(Information taken from the Catholic Encyclopedia, 1912 edition, Vol 13, pp. 580 - 581)

1) At the *First Provincial Council of Baltimore in 1829*, it was declared by the assembled Fathers to be "absolutely necessary that schools should be established, in which the young may be taught the principles of faith and morality, while being instructed in letters." This was the first authoritative declaration of the Church in the United States on the subject of Catholic Schools, and the decrees of subsequent councils have but reiterated, amplified or given more precise practical effect to the general law thus

laid down.

2) The *First Plenary Council of Baltimore, held in 1852,* exhorted the bishops "to see that schools be established in connection with all the churches of their dioceses", and if necessary, to provide for the support of the school from the revenues of the church to which the school was attached.

3) The *Second Plenary Council of Baltimore* simply ratified the decrees of the previous councils. In 1875, however, the *Congregation of Propaganda* issued an "Instruction to the Bishops of the United States concerning the Public Schools", in which it was pointed out that the public schools as conducted involved grave danger to the faith and morals of Catholic children, and that consequently both the natural and Divine law forbade the attendance of Catholic children at such schools, unless the proximate danger could be removed.

4) The *Third Plenary Council of Baltimore, held in 1884,* exhorted the faithful to send their children to the Catholic schools: "Therefore we not only exhort Catholic parents with paternal love, but we also command them with all of the authority in our power, to procure for their beloved offspring, given to them by God, reborn in Christ in Baptism, and destined for Heaven, a truly Christian and Catholic education, and to defend and safeguard them from the dangers of an education merely secular during the entire period of childhood and youth; and therefore to send them to parish schools or others truly Catholic, unless perchance the Ordinary, in a particular case, should judge that it might be permitted otherwise."

The Council issued the following decrees concerning Catholic schools:

a) "Near each church, a parochial school if it does not yet exist, is to be erected within two years from the promulgation of this Council, and it is to be maintained *in perpetuum*, unless the bishop, on account of grave difficulties, judges that a postponement be allowed."

b) "A priest who, by his grave negligence, prevents the erection of a school within this time or its maintenance, or who, after repeated admonitions of the bishop, does not attend to the matter, deserves removal from that church."

c) "A mission or a parish which so neglects to assist a priest in erecting or maintaining a school, that by reason of this supine negligence the school is rendered impossible, should be reprehended by the bishop and, by the most efficacious and prudent means possible, induced to contribute the necessary support."

d) "All Catholic parents are bound to send their children to the parochial schools, unless either at home or in other Catholic schools they may sufficiently and evidently provide for the Christian education of their children, or unless it be lawful to send them to other schools on account of a sufficient cause approved by the bishop, and with opportune cautions and remedies."

5) *Pope Leo XIII*, in a letter addressed to the American Hierarchy through Cardinal Gibbons in May, 1893, declared that the decrees of the Baltimore Councils were to be steadfastly observed in determining the attitude to be maintained by Catholics in respect both to parish and to public schools. (cf. The Catholic Encyclopedia, Vol 13, p. 583).

IV. Catholic Principles Governing Education

(Information taken from the Catholic Encyclopedia, 1912 edition, Vol 13, pp. 558 - 559)

I. General Principles:

1) The Church, being a perfect society, has the right to establish schools, which, although they may be permitted by the civil law merely as private institutions, are of their nature public;

2) By natural law, the obligation lies primarily with the parents of a child to provide his education (in the natural order), as well as for his physical support. This is part of the purpose and aim of the family as an institution. If no provision is made by any

other institution, the parents must provide education either by their own effort, or that of others whom they employ;

3) When the parents neglect their duty in the matter of education, the State, in the interests of the public welfare, takes up the obligation of teaching. It has, therefore, the right to establish schools and, consequently, the right to compel attendance insofar as the principle holds good that public welfare demands a knowledge, at least, of the elementary branches of education.

II. Particular Principles:

1) The Church has the exclusive right to teach religion to Catholic children. Neither the parents nor the State can exercise this right except they do with the consent (as parents do) and under the supervision and control of the ecclesiastical authorities.

2) The Church cannot approve schools which exclude religion from the curriculum, both because religion is the most important subject in education, and because even secular education is not possible in its best form unless religion be made the central, vitalizing and coordinating factor in the life of the child. The Church, sometimes, tolerates schools in which religion is not taught, and permits Catholic children to attend them, when the circumstances are such as to leave no alternative, and when due precautions are taken to supply by other means the religious training which such schools do not give. She reserves the right to judge whether this be the case, and, if her judgment is unfavorable, claims the right to forbid attendance.

3) In all schools, whether established by the Church or the State, or even by a group of families (so long as there are pupils received from different families) the State has the right to see that the laws of public health, public order, and public morality are observed, and if in any school doctrines were taught subversive of public peace or otherwise opposed to the interests of the general public, the State would have the right to intervene "in the name of the good of the general public."

4) State monopoly of education has been considered by the Church to be nothing short of a tyrannical usurpation. In principle,

it overrides the fundamental right of the parents, denies the right of the Church even to open and maintain schools for the teaching of religion alone, and in its natural effect on public opinion tends to place religion below considerations of mere worldly welfare.

5) The Church does not deny the right of the State to levy taxes for the support of the State schools, although this leads to injustice in the manner of its application is some countries. The principle is always distinct from the abuse of the principle. Similarly, the Church does not deny the right of the State to decree compulsory education so long as such decrees do not abrogate other and more fundamental rights. It should always be remembered, however, that compulsion on the part of the State is not the exercise of a primary and predominant right [for this belongs to the parents and to the Church], but must be justified by considerations of the public good.

6) Finally, the rights of the Church in the matter of religious teaching extend not only to the subject of religion itself, but to such matters as the character of the teacher, the spirit and tone of the teaching in such subjects as history and science, and the contents of the textbooks used. She recognizes that de-Christianized teaching and de-Christianized textbooks have inevitably the effect of lessening in the minds of pupils the esteem which she teaches them to have for religion. In a word, her rights are bounded not by the subject of religion, but by the spiritual interests of the children committed to her care.

FOOTNOTES

[1] Information taken from the Catholic Encyclopedia, 1912 edition, Vol 13, pp. 554-588, and from *The Philosophy of Education*, by Thomas E. Shields, 1917 edition, 446 pages.

[2] McCormick, *History of Education*, Washington, 1915, p. 24. (Quoted by Thomas Shields, *Philosophy of Education*, p. 326).

[3] Pope Pius XI, *Encyclical on Christian Education of Youth*, Dec. 31, 1929.

[4] See Thomas Shields, *Philosophy of Education*, ed. 1921, p. 292.

[5] Ibid, pp. 305-306.

[6] Ibid, p. 335.

[7] Ibid.

[8] Chrodegang, Bishop of Metz, 742-66, is said to be the founder of medieval cathedral schools, but only in the sense that he organized the clergy of his cathedral church into a community, and ordained that they undertake the conduct and management of the school attached to their church. (See the Catholic Encyclopedia, p. 556).

[9] Catholic Encyclopedia (1912 ed.), p. 556.

[10] Ibid.

[11] Ibid.

[12] See Thomas Shields, op. cit., pp. 335-336.

[13] Rev. George Stebbing, CSSR, *The Story of the Catholic Church*, pp. 219-220.

[14] Thomas Shields, op. cit.., p. 336.

[15] The Catholic Encyclopedia (1912 ed.), p. 556

[16] Ibid, p. 556

[17] Thomas Shields, op. cit., p. 372.

[18] Ibid, pp. 337-338.

[19] Catholic Encyclopedia (1912 ed.), pp. 579-580.

[20] Beecher also gave a series of anti-Catholic sermons near Charleston (a suburb of Boston) on Aug. 11, 1834. Following these sermons, the Ursuline Convent was set on fire and sacked by a mob. The cemetery was violated: graves were dug up, coffins were opened and their contents exposed.

Samuel F. B. Morse, inventor of the telegraph, in his very popular book, *Foreign Conspiracy*, urged Protestants to stop fighting among themselves and awake to the menace of Catholicism. He declared that they must unite against Catholic schools; throw out all Catholic office-holders; and terminate lenient immigration and naturalization laws. See Paul Fisher, *Behind the Lodge Door*, pp. 61-63.

[21] Thomas Shields, op. cit.., p. 343.

[22] Pope Pius XI, *Christian Education of Youth*, Dec. 31, 1929.

[23] Ibid.

[24] Ibid.

[25] Pope Pius XI, Letter to Cardinal Gasparri, May 30, 1929 (see *Papal Teachings on Education*, published by the Daughters of St. Paul, #237)

[26] Pope Pius XI, *Christian Education of Youth*, Dec. 31, 1929.

[27] Ibid.

[28] Pope Pius XI, May 24, 1925 (see *Papal Teachings on Education*, by the Daughters of St. Paul, #213).

In the Catholic Encyclopedia (1912 ed.), p. 556, we read: "We know that before the end of the ninth century, *both boys and girls* attended the schools attached to the parish churches in the Diocese of Soissons [France]."

[29] Pope Pius XI, May 14, 1929 (see *Papal Teachings on Education*, by the Daughters of St. Paul, #234).

[30] Pope Pius XII, Allocution of Oct. 26, 1941 (see *Papal Teachings on Education*, by the Daughters of St. Paul, # 416-417).

[31] Pope Pius XI, *Christian Education of Youth*, Dec. 31, 1929.

[32] Pope Pius IX, Nov. 24, 1875 (see *Papal Teachings on Education*, by the Daughters of St. Paul, # 61 - 63).

[33] Pope Pius XI, *Christian Education of Youth*, Dec. 31, 1929.

For more family books
and a free Angelus Press catalog

ANGELUS PRESS
2918 Tracy Avenue
Kansas City, Missouri 64109

1-800-96-ORDER
1-800-966-7337